The Only GLUTEN FREE CAKES & BAKES Recipes You'll Ever Need

The Cake & Bake Academy

First published in 2017 by Kyle Craig Publishing

Editor: Alison McNicol

Design: Julie Anson

With thanks to Frances Williams

ISBN: 978-1-78595-271-5
A CIP record for this book is available from the British Library.

A Kyle Craig Publication

www.kyle-craig.com

Contents

GLUTEN FREE ESSENTIALS INGREDIENTS

The following mixes can be used to replace store-bought gluten-free flours and ingredients – and can be used in many of the recipes in this book too!

GLUTEN FREE PLAIN FLOUR BLEND

Ingredients

240g/ 8½ oz rice flour
100g/ 3½ oz cornflour/ cornstarch,
30g/ 1½ oz tapioca starch/ tapioca flour
1 tsp xanthan gum

Method

To make one batch, combine all ingredients together and mix well. Store in a container with airtight lid. Stir before using.

GLUTEN FREE BAKING POWDER

Ingredients

1 tsp cream of tartar
½ tsp bicarbonate of soda/ baking soda

Method

Combine the cream of tartar with the bicarbonate of soda/ baking soda.

GLUTEN FREE SELF RAISING FLOUR

Ingredients

125g/ 4oz gluten free plain flour/ gluten free all-purpose flour
1 tsp cream of tartar
½ tsp bicarbonate of soda/ baking soda

Method

Combine the cream of tartar with the bicarbonate of soda/ baking soda to make gluten-free baking powder, as in the recipe above. Sift the baking powder into the gluten free flour and combine well. Store in a container with airtight lid. Stir before using.

PUMPKIN PIE SPICE

Ingredients

6 tbsp ground cinnamon
4 tsp ground ginger
3 tsp ground cloves
4 tsp ground nutmeg
3 tsp ground cloves
3 tsp ground allspice

Method

Combine all the spices and mix well and store in a jar or airtight container.

APPLE CAKE

Ingredients

675g/ 1½ lb green eating apples (granny smiths etc.)

240g/ 8½ oz plus 2 tbsp caster sugar

100g/ 3½ oz plus 2 tbsp plain/ all-purpose gluten-free flour

240ml/ 8 fl oz light olive oil or canola oil

240ml/ 8 fl oz whole milk/ full fat milk

1 large egg, plus 2 yolks

1 tbsp brandy

2 tsp gluten free baking powder

1 tsp lemon juice

25g/ 1oz almond flour

1 tsp pure vanilla essence

½ tsp salt

2½ tbsp sliced almonds

Method

Preheat the oven to 170C / 325F / Gas Mark 3

Line and grease a 23"/9" spring-form tin with grease-proof paper/ baking parchment and place on a baking tray.

Peel and core the apples and cut each into approx. 8-10 thin wedges, cover and microwave in 30 second bursts until tender and soft. Mix the brandy and lemon juice and trickle this over them and leave to cool for 20 minutes. Mix 100g/ 3½ oz of the flour blend, 240g/ 8½ oz of sugar and the almond flour in a large bowl then add the salt and baking powder. Add one large egg, milk, vanilla, oil and whisk until smooth. Set approximately ¼ of the mixture aside in a separate mixing bowl. Add the two egg yolks to the larger portion of the mixture and whisk in. Mix in the apple slices then tip the mixture into the prepared pan, smoothing the top with the back of a spoon.

Whisk 2 tbsp of the flour blend into remaining mixture and smooth it over the top of the tin. Sprinkle the top with 2 tbsp of caster sugar and the almonds. Bake for 60 – 75 minutes, when the cake should be set in the centre. Transfer tin to a wire rack to cool.

VANILLA SPONGE CAKE

Ingredients

175g/ 6oz gluten free plain/ all-purpose flour
200g/ 7oz caster sugar
240ml/ 8 fl oz light olive oil
240ml/ 8 fl oz water
1 tbsp vinegar or 1 tbsp orange juice
1 tsp gluten free baking powder
1 tsp bicarbonate of soda/ baking soda
1 tsp vanilla essence

Method

Preheat the oven to 180C / 350F / Gas Mark 4

Grease and line a 20cm/ 8" cake tin with grease-proof paper/ baking parchment.

Combine the flour, sugar, bicarbonate of soda/ baking soda and baking powder together in a large bowl.

In a separate small bowl, mix the oil, vinegar, vanilla and water together.

Make a dent in the flour mix and pour in the wet mix. Mix together slowly, then beat for a few minutes until a thick consistency.

Pour the mixture into the prepared tin and bake 45-60 minutes.

When cooked and the cake is just springy, remove to a wire rack for cooling — around 5-10 minutes — before turning out.

VICTORIA SPONGE CAKE

Ingredients

240g/ 8½ oz gluten free self-raising flour
240g/ 8½ oz caster sugar
240g/ 8½ oz butter
3 medium eggs
1 tsp icing sugar/ confectioners sugar
Seedless raspberry or strawberry jam/ preserve

Method

Preheat the oven to 180C / 350F / Gas Mark 4

Grease and line a 20cm/ 8" cake tin with grease-proof paper/ baking parchment.

Beat the butter and sugar by hand or electric mixer for 3-4 minutes until light and fluffy.

Gently beat in the eggs one by one with a tbsp of flour, then fold in remaining flour.

Pour mixture into the tin and tap the cake tin gently a few times to flatten out the top.

Bake for 35-40 minutes or until a skewer comes out clean.

Leave the cake in the tin for a few minutes before removing onto a rack to allow to cool entirely.

Cut the cake in half horizontally. Spread the jam/ preserve over the bottom section, then replace the top. Sieve with icing sugar/ confectioners sugar before serving. You may also choose to include a buttercream too, if desired.

CHOCOLATE FUDGE CAKE

Ingredients

CAKE:

225g/ 8oz good-quality (60% cocoa) dark chocolate
225g/ 8oz butter
100g/ 3½ oz gluten free plain/ all-purpose flour
225g/ 8oz light muscovado sugar
225g/ 8oz golden caster sugar/ golden superfine sugar
100g/ 3½ oz gluten free self-raising flour
30g/ 1½ oz cocoa powder
1 tsp instant coffee, mixed with 125ml/ 4 fl.oz cold water
1 tsp xanthan gum
½ tsp bicarbonate of soda/ baking soda
100ml/ 3½ fl oz buttermilk*
3 large eggs
100g/ 3½ oz shaved white or milk chocolate, for decoration

FUDGE GANACHE:

225g/ 8oz good-quality (60% cocoa) dark chocolate
60g/ 2oz dark muscovado sugar
225g/ 8oz butter
5 tbsp evaporated milk
½ tsp vanilla essence

Method

Preheat the oven to 170C / 325F / Gas Mark 3

Grease and line a 20cm/ 8" cake tin with grease-proof paper/ baking parchment. Gently melt the chocolate, butter and coffee mixture in the microwave on high for about 1½ minutes. Check and stir every 30 seconds.

In a large bowl combine the flours, bicarbonate of soda/ baking soda, sugars, cocoa powder and xanthan gum. Beat the eggs in a separate bowl and add the buttermilk. Add to the flour mixture along with the melted chocolate. Combine everything well to a runny texture. Pour mixture into your cake tin and bake for around 75 minutes or until a skewer comes out clean. Remove from oven and leave to cool before turning out.

For the fudge ganache, mix all ingredients in a heavy based pan, heating slowly, stirring continuously until everything has melted. Leave to cool and then chill for 60 minutes. Cut the cake horizontally and sandwich the two halves together with a third of the ganache. Cover the top and sides with the rest then sprinkle with shaved chocolate to decorate.

**To make your own buttermilk, simply sour some milk by adding some acid. Pour 250ml milk into a jug and stir in one 15ml tablespoon of lemon juice or white wine vinegar. Stir well and leave to stand for 5 minutes before using as directed in the recipe. Full fat (whole) milk works best.*

LEMON DRIZZLE CAKE

Ingredients

175g/ 6oz gluten free self-raising flour, sieved
175g/ 6oz caster sugar/ superfine sugar
175g/ 6oz butter
2 large eggs
2 lemons, rind grated then set aside for juicing
2½ tbsp icing sugar/ confectioners sugar

Method

Preheat the oven to 180C / 350F / Gas Mark 4

Grease and line an 18cm/ 7" loaf tin with grease-proof paper/ baking parchment.

In a large bowl, beat the butter with the sugar until it is light and fluffy. Lightly beat in the eggs with 1 tbsp of flour and then fold the rest of the flour in. Add all the lemon rind plus the juice of ½ a lemon.

Pour the mixture into the tin and bake for 45 minutes or until a skewer comes out clean. Remove from the oven, allow to cool for 5 minutes then turn out onto a wire rack and allow to cool completely.

Mix the icing sugar/ confectioners sugar in a small bowl and stir in 4-6 tsp lemon juice so icing is spreadable. Pierce the cool cake with a small skewer and spread the icing over the top. Leave it to set before serving.

SCONES

Ingredients

125g/ 4oz gluten free plain flour/ gluten free all-purpose flour
125ml/ 4 fl oz milk, plus extra for brushing
60ml/ 2 fl oz cream
2 tsp baking powder
30g/ 1½ oz white rice flour
30g/ 1½ oz ground almonds
Pinch of salt

Method

Preheat the oven to 220C / 425F / Gas Mark 7

Line a baking tray with grease-proof paper/ baking parchment.

Combine the flour, almonds, baking powder and salt in a bowl.

Blend the milk and cream and pour into the middle of the flour mixture and mix until the dough forms.

Lightly flour your surface and gently roll the dough out until approximately 2.5cm/ 1" thick. Cut out rounds using a cutter. Continue until all dough is used.

Place the rounds on the baking tray and lightly brush tops with milk. Bake for 10 minutes or until risen and golden.

Whilst still warm pull apart and serve with strawberry jam/ preserve and whipped cream or butter, as desired.

BERRY COBBLER

Ingredients

400g/ 14oz of a variety of berries:
strawberries, blackberries, etc.
125g/ 4oz gluten free plain/ all-purpose flour
60g/ 2oz butter
1 tsp vanilla essence
2 tsp sugar
Honey or Maple syrup

Method

Preheat the oven to 190C / 375F / Gas Mark 5

Grease a large baking dish.

Place berries in the bottom of the baking dish.

Mix the flour, butter and vanilla by hand and use your fingers to make a crumbly topping. Add in the sugar and work through.

Sprinkle the crumble topping evenly over the berries.

Place in oven and cook for 25-35 minutes until top in golden.

Before serving, drizzle with organic honey or maple syrup.

STICKY TOFFEE PUDDING

Ingredients

PUDDING:

180g/6oz gluten free plain / all-purpose flour - plus extra for the moulds
250g/ 9oz dates, pitted and chopped
150g/ 5½ oz light brown sugar
100g/ 3½ oz butter
100ml/ 3½ fl oz milk
3 large eggs
2 tbsp maple syrup
1 tsp bicarbonate of soda/ baking soda
1 tsp baking powder
1 tsp vanilla essence
pinch sea salt

TOFFEE SAUCE:

175g/ 6oz light brown sugar
100g/ 3½ oz butter
230ml/ 8oz cream, plus extra thickened cream to serve
100ml/ 3½ fl oz maple syrup
1 tbsp black treacle/ molasses
½ tsp vanilla essence
pinch of sea salt

Method

Preheat the oven to 180C / 350F / Gas Mark 4

Grease and flour 6-8 dariole moulds and then line the bases with a disc of oiled baking paper/ parchment paper.

Soak the dates in boiling water for five minutes and then blend in a food processor until a smooth consistency. Add all the other pudding ingredients and mix until well combined.

Spoon the mixture into the prepared moulds about ¾ way up and bake for 20 minutes until risen and firm or until a skewer comes out clean.

Whilst the puddings are baking, make the toffee sauce. Melt the butter, maple syrup and treacle/ molasses pan over low heat and simmer for a 2-3 minutes. Gradually stir in the vanilla, cream and salt and bring to the boil for 1–2 minutes or until slightly thickened.

Leave the puddings to cool in their moulds for a few minutes. Turn them out onto serving dishes and spoon the warm toffee sauce over the top. Serve with a little thickened cream.

RED VELVET CAKE

Ingredients

CAKE:

300g/ 11oz gluten free plain / all-purpose flour
300g/ 11oz sugar
360ml/ 12 fl oz vegetable oil
240ml/ 8 fl oz buttermilk*
2 large eggs
2 tsp red food colouring
1 tsp bicarbonate of soda/ baking soda
1 tsp cocoa powder
1 tsp white distilled vinegar
1 tsp vanilla essence

FROSTING:

400g/ 14oz icing sugar/ confectioners sugar
100g/3½ oz shortening
30ml/ 1 fl oz water
½ tbsp vanilla essence
Pinch of salt

Method

Preheat the oven to 180C / 350F / Gas Mark 4

Grease and flour three 23cm/ 9" round cake pans. In a large mixing bowl sieve the flour, bicarbonate of soda/ baking soda, sugar, salt and cocoa. In a separate bowl mix the buttermilk, eggs, oil, food colouring, vinegar and vanilla. Combine both bowls and mix to form a smooth consistency.

Divide the cake mixture evenly among the three prepared cake pans and bake for about 30 minutes, or until a skewer comes out clean. Remove from oven and turn onto cooling racks. Once cakes have cooled, mix the icing sugar/ confectioners sugar, shortening, vanilla and salt. Gently add in water until you get a thick smooth consistency.

Level then frost the top of two cakes with 1/3 of the icing for each. Layer all three cakes together. Use the rest of the frosting to cover the top.

**To make your own buttermilk, simply sour some milk by adding some acid. Pour 250ml milk into a jug and stir in one 15ml tablespoon of lemon juice or white wine vinegar. Stir well and leave to stand for 5 minutes before using as directed in the recipe. Full fat (whole) milk works best.*

APPLE CRUMBLE

Ingredients

6-8 green apples, cored and peeled
175g/ 6oz sugar + 2 tbsp extra
1½ tbsp butter, softened
4 tbsp rice flour
3 tbsp almond meal
2 tbsp desiccated coconut

Method

Preheat the oven to 180C / 350F / Gas Mark 4

Grease a medium ovenproof dish.

Slice each apple into approximately 8-10 wedges and put in a pan with a little water. On a low to medium heat, cook until the apples are tender.

Combine all topping ingredients and rub together with fingers to make a crumbly texture.

Layer the apples and their juices in the ovenproof dish. Cover the apples with the crumble mixture, sprinkle with the 2 tbsp of sugar and bake for 30-35 minutes or until golden brown.

BASIC PANCAKES

Ingredients

PANCAKES:

200g / 7oz gluten free self-raising flour
75g/ 3oz brown sugar
40g/ 1½ oz butter, melted
300ml/ 10 fl oz buttermilk*
125ml/ 4 fl oz single cream/ thin cream
1 egg, lightly beaten
1 tbsp caster sugar/ superfine sugar

CHOCOLATE SAUCE:

100g/ 3½ oz dark chocolate
(minimum 70% cocoa solids)
125 ml/ 4 fl.oz double cream/ thick cream
1 tbsp golden syrup/ corn syrup
2 tsp espresso coffee
2 tbsp water

Method

Mix together the flour and sugar in a large bowl and make a well in the centre. Add the egg and buttermilk and stir to combine until you have a thick batter.

Grease a large non-stick frying pan/ skillet with a little of the butter. Place over medium-low heat. Use a large spoon to pour enough batter for each round pancake. Cook for 2 minutes or until bubbles appear on the surface. Turn and cook until golden. Transfer to a plate. Repeat for other pancakes.

To makes the sauce, break up the chocolate and place into a heavy-based saucepan. Add the hot coffee with the remaining ingredients and gently heat until all melts.

Ready to serve with pancakes.

**To make your own buttermilk, simply sour some milk by adding some acid. Pour 250ml milk into a jug and stir in one 15ml tablespoon of lemon juice or white wine vinegar. Stir well and leave to stand for 5 minutes before using as directed in the recipe. Full fat (whole) milk works best.*

COCONUT FLOUR PANCAKES

Ingredients

60g/ 2oz coconut flour
180ml/ 6fl.oz single cream/ thin cream
60ml/ 2fl.oz whole / full fat milk
4 large eggs, room temperature
2 tsp vanilla essence
1 tsp bicarbonate of soda/ baking soda
1 tbsp honey
½ tsp sea salt
butter for frying

Method

Preheat frying pan/ griddle over medium-low heat.

Beat the eggs until frothy and combine with the honey and vanilla in a small bowl.

In a medium-sized bowl mix coconut flour, bicarbonate of soda/ baking soda, and salt.

Gradually stir in ¾ of wet mixture into dry ingredients, until coconut flour is incorporated so it has a thick consistency. Allow to rest for 5 minutes.

Grease a large non-stick frying pan/ skillet with a little of the butter. Place over a medium-low heat. Ladle a few tbsp of batter into pan for each pancake and flatten slightly. Aim for a pancake around 5cm/ 2" across and reasonably thick.

Cook for a few minutes on each side, until the tops bubble and the bottoms start to brown. Turn and cook an additional 2-3 minutes. Repeat.

EASY CHOCOLATE MOUSSE CAKE

Ingredients

100g/ 3½ oz unsalted butter
4 large eggs, at room temperature
240g/ 8½ oz dark chocolate
(min. 60% cocoa solids)
2 tbsp sugar

Method

Preheat the oven to 200C / 400F / Gas Mark 6

Grease and line an 8"/ 20cm round spring-form cake tin with grease-proof paper/ baking parchment. Wrap the bottom of the pan with a double layer of foil. Place a roasting tin on the center rack of the oven.

Combine chocolate and butter in a heatproof bowl set over a saucepan of simmering water and stir gently until melted and smooth. Set aside to cool.

Whisk the eggs until very foamy – by hand or electric mixer. Gradually add sugar and continue to beat until thick and pale in colour. Add half of the eggs to the chocolate and fold in gently. Add the remaining eggs gradually and continue to fold in until fully blended.

Pour mixture into the pan and put in the roasting tin. Pour boiling water into the roasting tin approximately 1.5cm/½" up the sides of the cake tin. Bake for 5 minutes, then turn down to 180°C/ 350°F and bake for about 30 minutes until firm or until a skewer comes out virtually clean.

Put tin on to a wire rack to cool completely before turning out. Dust with cocoa and serve.

RASPBERRY LOAF CAKE

Ingredients

CAKE:

175g/ 6oz caster sugar/ superfine sugar
175g/ 6oz unsalted butter, at room temperature
125g/ 4oz rice flour
3 large eggs
1 tsp gluten free baking powder
60g/ 2oz ground almonds
1 tsp vanilla essence
10-12 fresh raspberries

FROSTING:

200g/ 7oz cream cheese
100g/ 3½ oz icing sugar/ confectioners sugar, sieved
60g/ 2oz butter, softened
Fresh raspberries to decorate

Method

Preheat the oven to 180C / 350F / Gas Mark 4

Line and grease a 900g/ 2lb loaf tin with grease-proof paper/ baking parchment.

Beat the butter and sugar until pale in colour and fluffy in texture.

Whisk in the eggs one at a time and then add the baking powder, almonds and rice flour. Combine well.

Pour mixture into the tin and smooth the top gently. Drop the fresh raspberries into the mixture and spread equally through.

Bake for 30-35 minutes or until a skewer comes out clean. Leave the cake to cool on a wire rack before turning out.

Make the frosting by beating the butter and icing sugar/ confectioners sugar together and then beat in the cream cheese. Spread over the top of the cooled cake with a palette knife/ spatula and decorate with fresh raspberries to serve.

FARMHOUSE CAKE

Ingredients

275g/ 10oz currants
225g/ 8oz sultanas
165g/ 5½ oz gluten free plain / all-purpose flour
125g/ 4oz glace cherries/ candied cherries, chopped
125g/ 4oz mixed peel, chopped
100g/ 3½ oz ground almonds
75g/ 3oz cornflour/ cornstarch
225g/ 8oz butter, room temperature
250g/ 9oz golden syrup/ corn syrup
4 large eggs
½ tsp gluten free baking powder
1¾ tsp mixed spice

Method

Preheat the oven to 170C / 325F / Gas Mark 3
Grease and line a 23cm/ 9" cake tin with grease-proof paper/ baking parchment.

Beat the butter and golden syrup/ corn syrup until light and fluffy and then beat in the eggs one at a time. Mix in all the dried fruit.

Sieve together the flour, cornflour/ cornstarch, almond, baking powder and mixed spice and fold into the batter.

Pour into the cake tin and level the top.

Bake for 75-90 minutes until firm to touch and a skewer inserted comes out clean.

Leave to cool on a wire rack.

CARROT AND WALNUT BUNDT CAKE

Ingredients

250g/ 9oz sugar
240g/ 8½ oz almond flour
125g/ 4oz carrots, grated
100g/ 3½ oz chopped walnuts
2 large eggs plus 3 egg whites
60g/ 2oz cornflour/ cornstarch
1 tsp finely grated orange zest
¾ tsp ground cinnamon
¾ tsp ground ginger
½ tsp salt
Icing sugar/ confectioners sugar to decorate

Method

Preheat the oven to 190C / 375F / Gas Mark 5

Grease a 25cm/ 10" Bundt pan.

Mix the 2 large eggs and 200g/ 7oz of the sugar in a large bowl and then beat until pale and thick, by hand or using an electric mixer.

Whisk together the flour, cornflour/ cornstarch, spices, orange zest and salt in a large bowl and stir in the shredded carrots.

Gently fold the wet ingredients into the carrot mixture and add in the chopped walnuts.

In another bowl beat the egg whites until just starting to foam. Add the rest of the sugar and then beat again until you have stiff and shiny peaks forming. This should take about 8 minutes.

Slowly and gradually fold the beaten egg mixture into the carrot mixture until just combined and then pour into the pan.

Bake for 25-30 minutes until just springy or until a skewer comes out clean. Transfer to a wire rack for cooling before turning out.

Lightly serve topped with sieved icing sugar/ confectioners sugar.

DARK CHOCOLATE FUDGE BROWNIES

Ingredients

240g/ 8½ oz golden caster sugar/
golden superfine sugar
240g/ 8½ oz plain/dark chocolate
125g/ 4oz gluten free self-raising flour, sieved
150g/ 5oz butter, cubed
4 large eggs
1tbsp cocoa powder

Method

Preheat the oven to 180C / 350F / Gas Mark 4

Line and grease a tin 27cm x 17.5cm x 3.5cm/ 10½ " x 7" x 1½ " with baking paper/ baking parchment.

Break 200g/ 7oz of the chocolate into a glass bowl, add the butter and place this over a pan of simmering water to melt. Once done so, put aside.

Chop the remaining chocolate into small pieces and set aside. Whisk the sugar and eggs together in a large bowl using an electric hand mixer, until thick, pale, fluffy and voluminous. Pour in the cooled melted chocolate, and gently fold mixture together. Add the sifted flour and the cocoa powder bit by bit, folding again. Finally stir in the remaining chocolate.

Pour the mixture into the tin and spread it out evenly. Bake for around 20-23 minutes, or until a skewer comes out clean and the top is crusty.

Remove from the oven and leave to cool in the tray.

BLUEBERRY MUFFINS

Ingredients

MUFFINS:
250g/ 9oz gluten free plain / all-purpose flour
165g/ 5½ oz blueberries
150g/ 5oz sugar
125g/ 4oz unsalted butter, melted and cooled
120ml/ 4fl oz whole milk/ full fat milk
2 large eggs
2 tsp lemon zest, finely grated
1½ tsp baking powder
1 tsp xanthan gum
1 tsp vanilla essence
½ tsp salt

FROSTING:
200g/ 7oz cream cheese
100g/ 3½ oz icing sugar/ confectioners sugar, sieved
60g/ 2oz butter, softened
Extra blueberries for decoration

Method

Preheat the oven to 190C / 375F / Gas Mark 5

Lightly grease a 12-cup muffin tin or line with paper liners.

Mix the sugar, flour, xantham gum, baking powder and salt in a bowl.

Whisk the milk, eggs, butter, lemon zest and vanilla in another bowl until combined.

Stir the wet ingredients into the flour mixture. Fold in the blueberries and be careful not to over stir. Divide the mixture between the muffin cases, filling to around ½ full.

Bake for around 20 minutes until muffins are golden or until a skewer comes out clean. Leave to cool in the tin on a wire rack.

To make the frosting, with an electric whisk, beat the butter, cream cheese and icing sugar/ confectioners sugar until a smooth consistency.

Pipe or spoon on top of each muffin and add fresh blueberries to decorate before serving.

RAISIN OATMEAL MUFFINS

Ingredients

125g/ 4oz gluten free plain / all-purpose flour
100g/ 3½ oz gluten free oats
150g/ 5oz brown sugar
150g/ 5oz raisins
180ml/ 6 fl oz applesauce
100g/ 3½ oz butter
1 egg
2 tbsp cornflour/ cornstarch
1 tsp gluten free baking powder
½ tsp bicarbonate of soda/ baking soda
½ tsp salt
¾ tsp cinnamon

Method

Preheat the oven to 180C / 350F / Gas Mark 4

Lightly grease a muffin tin or line with paper liners.

In a bowl, beat the butter and sugar together until a creamy texture. Then beat in the egg.

Gradually add the flour, sugar, baking powder, cornflour/ cornstarch, bicarbonate of soda/ baking soda, salt and cinnamon and stir through.

Then mix in the raisins.

Divide the mixture between the muffin cases filling around ½ full.

Bake for approximately 22 minutes or until golden and risen. Leave to cool in the tin on a wire rack.

CINNAMON BUNS

Ingredients

DOUGH:
600g/ 1lb 5oz gluten-free flour blend
125g/ 4oz + 1 tbsp sugar, divided
175ml/ 6fl oz milk
125g/ 4oz salted butter, cubed
100ml/ 3½ fl oz warm water
2 packets active dry yeast
3 large eggs,
2 tsp xanthan gum
1½ tsp salt

FILLING:
165g/ 5½ oz sugar
60g/ 2oz salted butter, melted
3 tbsp ground cinnamon

Method

Preheat the oven to 180C / 350F / Gas Mark 4

Grease a 33cm x 22cm x 5cm/ 13 x 9 x 2" baking tin.

For the dough, heat the milk in a pan until just starts to bubble. Then remove from heat. Stir in 125g/ 4oz sugar, salt and the butter. Let the butter melt then allow it to cool down.

Mix the warm water, 1 tbsp of sugar and the yeast together. Let it stand until starts to foam then add the warm milk mixture and eggs to this. Mix slowly by hand or electric mixer until blended and then add the flour and xanthan gum. Continue mixing until a dough is formed that is soft and pliable but not sticky.

On a lightly floured surface, roll out the dough to around 61cm x 41cm /24" x 1" in size. Trim the edges to make a rectangle. For the filling, brush the dough with melted butter. Combine the sugar and cinnamon and sprinkle this over the buttered dough. Roll the dough up to form a 60cm/ 24"roll and cut in approximately 4cm/ 1½ " slices. Pinch each bun to seal and place them on the tin, cover and let rest for 30 minutes.

Bake the rolls for 25-30 minutes, until golden. Remove from oven and cool.

CHOCOLATE CHUNK COOKIES

Ingredients

300g/ 11oz semi-sweet chocolate chunks/chips
275g/ 10oz Gluten-Free Flour Blend
140g/ 4½ oz brown sugar
100g/ 3½ oz sugar
175g/ 6oz butter, softened
2 large eggs
2 tsp vanilla
1 tsp gluten free baking powder
1 tsp bicarbonate of soda/ baking soda
½ tsp salt

Method

Preheat the oven to 190C / 375F / Gas Mark 5

Mix the flour, bicarbonate of soda/ baking soda, baking powder and salt together in a medium bowl.

In another bowl beat the butter and both sugars together with an electric mixer at medium speed until creamy. Add eggs and vanilla and continue beating, until well combined.

Add the flour mixture slowly and gradually, beating at a low speed until well combined. Then stir in the chocolate chips.

Use two tablespoons to put the mixture onto an ungreased baking tray, around 5cm/ 2" apart. Bake for 8-12 minutes or until just golden brown.

Cool for a couple of minutes on the baking tray and then remove with a slice to a wire rack to cool completely. You may then choose to drizzle with icing/frosting for extra decadence!

GINGER COOKIES

Ingredients

375g/ 13oz gluten free plain / all-purpose flour
200g/ 7oz light brown soft sugar
125g/ 4oz butter
100g/ 3½ oz golden syrup/ corn syrup
30g/ 1½ oz fresh ginger, peeled and grated
1 large egg, beaten
1 tbsp ground ginger
1 tsp bicarbonate of soda/ baking soda

Method

Preheat the oven to 180C / 350F / Gas Mark 4

Line two baking trays with baking paper/ baking parchment.

Melt the butter with the golden syrup/ corn syrup in a small pan and set aside to cool completely.

Mix the flour, sugar, baking powder, bicarbonate of soda/ baking soda and ground ginger into a mixing bowl.

Add the butter and golden syrup/ corn syrup to the mixture and then add the egg. Whisk to combine the ingredients. It will start to form a wet dough. Leave aside to cool for about 30 mins.

Take a piece of dough and roll into a small ball around the size of a walnut and flatten them gently onto your baking tray. Leave a decent size gap between each one. Bake for approximately 10-20 minutes or until they are golden in colour and slightly risen. Reduce oven temperature to 130C/ 275F/ Gas Mark 1 and continue baking for around 15-20 minutes more. Remove from oven and leave to cool on their trays.

SALTED PISTACHIO NUTELLA COOKIES

Ingredients

175g/ 6oz buckwheat flour
60g/ 2oz white rice flour
60g/ 2oz gluten free plain flour/ gluten free all-purpose flour
100g/ 3½ oz dark brown sugar
60g/ 2oz granulated sugar
240g/ 8½ oz semi-sweet or dark chocolate
240ml/ 8fl oz Nutella/ chocolate hazelnut spread
120g/ 4oz butter
75g/ 3oz unsalted pistachios, shelled and chopped
2 large eggs
1 tbsp vanilla essence
1 tsp gluten free baking powder
¼ tsp salt
Salt for sprinkling

Method

Preheat the oven to 180C / 350F / Gas Mark 4

Line a baking tray with grease-proof paper/ baking parchment.

Melt the butter in small pan and pour into a large mixing bowl. Add sugars and stir until combined. Mix in the eggs and vanilla. Melt the chocolate hazelnut spread in a microwave for approximately 10-20 seconds. Pour this into the bowl and mix until completely combined.

Add flours, baking powder and salt and mix well until it forms a dough. Place dough in the fridge for 20-30 minutes. Roll dough into small balls around the size of a walnut and flatten each gently onto your baking tray. Leave a decent size gap between each one.

Bake for 8-10 minutes until the edges start to look baked. Let cool on the baking sheet for 1 minute before removing to a wire rack to cool completely.

Prepare another baking sheet with grease-proof paper/parchment.

Melt the chocolate and dip cookies halfway into the chocolate, shake, and place on the paper. Sprinkle with salt and the pistachios. Allow to set.

STRAWBERRY VANILLA CHEESECAKE

Ingredients

250g/9oz gluten-free digestive biscuits crumbs/ graham cracker crumbs
100g/ 3½ oz icing sugar/ confectioners sugar
650g/ 1lb 7oz soft cream cheese
300ml/ 10 fl oz double cream/ heavy cream
100g/ 3½ oz butter, melted
1½ tsp vanilla essence
Fresh strawberries for topping

Method

Preheat the oven to 180C / 350F / Gas Mark 4

Butter and line a 23cm/ 9" loose-bottomed round tin with baking paper/ parchment.

Put the biscuit/cracker crumbs in a bowl, then add the melted butter. Combine thoroughly until all the crumbs are completely coated. Transfer the mixture to a prepared tin and use the back of a spoon to press it down – then chill in the fridge for around 60 minutes.

Place the icing sugar/ confectioners sugar, soft cheese and vanilla essence in a clean bowl, then beat by hand or electric mixer until smooth. Gradually add in the double cream/ heavy cream and continue beating until the mixture is completely combined.

Spoon the cheesecake mixture onto the biscuit base and smooth out the top. Leave to set in the fridge, ideally overnight.

About 45 minutes before serving, remove from fridge and gently onto a serving plate. Add fresh strawberries to decorate.

BAKED VANILLA CHEESECAKE

Ingredients

BASE:
240g/ 8½ oz gluten-free porridge/rolled oats
60g/ 2oz caster/superfine sugar
100g/ 3½ oz butter
5 tbsp golden/light corn syrup

FILLING:
140g/ 4½ oz caster/superfine sugar
650g/ 1lb 7oz soft cream cheese
400ml/ 14 fl oz sour cream
240ml/ 8 fl oz extra thick double cream/ extra thick heavy cream
4 large eggs
2 tbsp icing sugar/ confectioners sugar
1 vanilla pod, split

Method

Preheat the oven to 170C / 325F / Gas Mark 3

Butter and line a 23cm/ 9" loose-bottomed round tin with baking paper/ baking parchment.

For the base, put the butter and syrup in a large saucepan and melt over a low heat. Mix the oats and sugar in and combine thoroughly.

Stir in the oats and sugar, ensuring all the oats are coated. Transfer to the prepared tin and use the back of a spoon to press it down. Place in fridge to cool and set.

In a large mixing bowl add the soft cheese, cream cheese, heavy cream, eggs, sugar, seeds from the vanilla pod. Whisk all together until fluffy.

Pour the mixture into the tin and on top of your base. Bake in the oven for 60-75 minutes until the cheesecake is set but slightly wobbly.

Cool completely in the tin on a wire rack, then chill in the fridge before serving.

PUMPKIN SPICE CHEESECAKE

Ingredients

BASE:

165g/ 5½ oz gluten-free digestive biscuit crumbs/ graham cracker crumbs
5 tbsp butter, unsalted, softened
½ tsp cinnamon
2 tsp icing/ confectioner's sugar

FILLING:

450g/ 1lb soft cream cheese, at room temperature
425g/ 15oz pumpkin puree, fresh or can
120ml/ 4 fl oz sour cream, light
4 large eggs, room temperature
4-6 tsp icing/ confectioner's sugar
1 tsp pumpkin pie spice (see recipe on p4)
2 tsp vanilla essence
1 tsp nutmeg
½ tsp cinnamon
½ tsp ground ginger
¼ tsp salt

Method

Preheat the oven to 180C / 350F / Gas Mark 4

Butter and line a 23cm/ 9" loose-bottomed round tin with baking paper/ baking parchment.

Mix together the biscuit / cracker crumbs, cinnamon, butter, and icing sugar.

Transfer the mixture to the prepared tin and use the back of a spoon to press it down.

Bake for 10 minutes. Set aside.

Reduce oven temperature to 150C / 300F / Gas Mark 2.

Beat cream cheese until smooth, by hand or using an electric mixer. Add the sour cream, eggs, pumpkin puree, icing sugar, vanilla essence and all remaining spices and blend until smooth.

Tip this filling into the crust and bake for 40-45 minutes until set but still wobbly. Turn off oven and allow to sit in oven for 2 hours, do not open or it will crack!

After 2 hours, remove and allow to finish cooling in tin on a wire rack.

APPLE PIE

Ingredients

PASTRY:
225g/ 8oz gluten free plain / all-purpose flour
125g/ 4oz unsalted butter
2 tbsp granulated sugar
4 tbsp cold water
1 large egg
Milk for brushing pastry

FILLING:
900g/ 2lb Bramley apples/ cooking apples
150g/ 5oz golden caster sugar/ golden superfine sugar
2½ tbsp gluten free cornflour/ cornstarch
1 tsp ground cinnamon

Method

Preheat the oven to 200C / 400F / Gas Mark 6

Grease and line a 23cm/ 9" pie dish.

Using your fingers, rub the butter and flour together in a large bowl until it become crumbly, then mix in the sugar. In another bowl, beat the water and egg then combine with the butter, flour, sugar mix until it forms a pastry dough. Wrap in in clingflim/ plastic wrap and let it rest for around 20-30 minutes.

In a large mixing bowl combine the golden caster sugar, cornflour and cinnamon. Peel the apples, then chop into thin wedges and chunks. Add the apples in with the sugar mixture, tossing to coat thoroughly.

Halve your dough and roll out evenly on a lightly floured surface. Cut a round large enough for the base, then repeat for the lid. Transfer one round into the base and then add the apple mix. Top with the second pastry round. Trim and seal the edges, then cut two air slits on the pastry lid. Brush a little milk on the top.

Bake the pie for 30-45 minutes or until the pastry is golden.

Remove from oven and let cool for 15 minutes before slicing and serving.

CHERRY PIE

Ingredients

PASTRY:

375g/ 13oz gluten free plain/ all-purpose flour, plus 1 tbsp sprinkling
60g/ 2oz icing sugar/ confectioners sugar
150g/ 5oz unsalted butter, cubed and chilled
120ml/ 4 fl oz ice water
1 egg white
½ tsp gluten free baking powder
½ tsp salt
¾ tsp xanthan gum

FILLING:

900g/ 2lb cherries, pitted
225g/ 8oz sugar
2 tbsp cornflour/ cornstarch
½ tsp cinnamon
pinch of salt

Method

Preheat the oven to 180C / 350F / Gas Mark 4

Grease and line a 23cm/9" pie dish.

To make the pastry, mix all the dry ingredients well. Add the butter and rub this in using your fingertips until the mixture resembles breadcrumbs. Gradually add the water and mix until a dough forms that's smooth and pliable. Wrap in clingfilm/ plastic wrap and chill.

For the filling, put 250g/ 9oz cherries, cinnamon, cornflour/ cornstarch and salt and in a pan. Mix well and cook on a medium heat for 7-8 minutes, always stirring. Remove from the heat, add the remaining cherries and combine well.

Halve your dough and roll out evenly on a lightly floured surface. Cut a round large enough for the base, then repeat for the lid. Transfer one round into the base and then add the cherry mix. Top with the second pastry round. Trim and seal the edges, then cut two air slits on the pastry lid. Brush a little milk on the top.

Bake the pie for 30-45 minutes or until the pastry is golden.

Remove from oven and let cool for 15 minutes before slicing and serving.

PUMPKIN PIE

Ingredients

CRUST:

120g/ 4oz white rice flour
60g/ 2oz tapioca flour
60g/ 2oz gluten free cornflour/cornstarch
6 tbsp butter, chilled and cubed
1 large egg
1 tbsp cider
½ tsp salt
3-4 tbsp iced water

FILLING:

300g/ 11oz sugar
800g/ 1¾ lb pumpkin puree, fresh or can
720ml/ 24 fl oz evaporated milk
4 large eggs, beaten
2 tsp ground cinnamon
1 tsp ground ginger
½ tsp ground cloves
¾ tsp salt

Method

Preheat the oven to 220C / 425F / Gas Mark 7

Grease and line a 23cm/ 9" pie dish.

For the crust, in a medium bowl mix the flours, cornflour/ cornstarch and salt together. Add the butter and work through with fingertips until the mixture resembles breadcrumbs. In the middle, add the egg and cider and stir gently until just mixed. Sprinkle water and then mix together by hand until it forms a firm but pliable dough ball.

Roll out your dough evenly on a lightly floured surface, to approximately 0.5cm/ ¼" thickness. Carefully place in bottom of pie dish.
Trim excess crust.

For the filling, combine the sugar, salt, and spices in bowl. Gradually add the eggs, mixing well, then add the pumpkin, sugar and spices. Stir in the evaporated gradually. Pour into your pie shell.

Bake for 15 minutes. Reduce temperature to 180C / 350F / Gas Mark 4 and bake for 45-50 minutes more, or until skewer inserted near center comes out clean.

Cool on wire rack completely before serving.

PEAR & ALMOND TART

Ingredients

CRUST:

150g/ 5oz gluten free plain / all-purpose flour
100g/ 3oz butter, chilled and cubed
1 large egg, beaten
1 tbsp icing sugar/ confectioners sugar
¼ tsp salt

FILLING:

140g/ 4½ oz butter, at room temperature
400g/ 14oz caster sugar/ superfine sugar
140g/ 4½ oz ground almonds
4 large pears
2 large eggs
1 tbsp cornflour/ cornstarch
1 tsp golden syrup/ corn syrup
1 cinnamon stick*
1 star anise*
4 cloves*
Half a lemon

Method

Preheat the oven to 190C / 375F / Gas Mark 5

Grease a 24cm-26cm/ 9"-10" tart tin.

For the pastry, rub the butter and flour together. Then add the icing/ confectioners sugar and salt until the mixture resembles breadcrumbs.

Gradually add ¾ of the beaten egg, mixing thoroughly until the dough is firm. Cover in cling film/plastic wrap and chill for around 25 minutes, then roll out evenly on a lightly floured surface. Cut a circle large enough to cover the bottom and sides of tin, press down and trim excess crust. Prick the base.

For the filling, beat the butter and 150g/ 5oz of the caster sugar/ superfine sugar. Beat in the eggs one by one. Fold in the cornflour/ cornstarch and then the almonds.

In a large pan put the 250g/9oz caster / superfine sugar with 450ml/ 15 fl oz of water. Heat gently until sugar has dissolved. Peel and cut 2 of the pears into small chunks and add to the pan with the spices* and lemon. Cover and simmer gently for 5-6 minutes. Remove and leave to cool for 10 minutes. Remove the spices* and lemon half from the mixture.

Take the filling and pour into tart tin and smooth out. Slice the other 2 pears thinly and place slices on top of the filling and fan around, overlapping in design. Drizzle the tart with golden syrup. Bake for 55-60 minutes or until tart is golden.

LEMON BARS

Ingredients

CRUST:
140g/ 4½ oz brown rice flour
140g/ 4½ gluten free cornflour/ cornstarch
240g/ 8½ oz unsalted butter,
room temperature
60g/ 2oz icing sugar/ confectioners sugar
2-3 tbsp milk
1 tsp vanilla essence
¼ tsp salt

FILLING:
600g/ 1lb 5oz sugar
125g/ 4oz gluten free plain / all-purpose flour
240ml/ 8 fl oz lemon juice
7 large eggs, room temperature
2 tbsp lemon zest, grated
Icing sugar/ confectioners sugar, for dusting

Method

Preheat the oven to 180C / 350F / Gas Mark 4

Line and grease a 23cm x 33cm x 5cm/ 9 x 13 x 2" baking tray.

For the crust, whisk together the flour, sugar and salt and butter in a medium bowl. Mix by hand or electric mixer until dough forms. Add extra milk if too dry.

Put dough into greased tray and spread evenly. Bake for 15-20 minutes until just browned. Remove and cool on wire rack. Increase oven temp to 190C / 375F / Gas Mark 5.

For the filling, mix the sugar and flour. Add the lemon juice and zest and eggs and whisk together well. Pour over cooled crust and bake for 25-30 minutes or until filling is set.

Remove and leave to cool. Dust with icing sugar/confectioners sugar before cutting and serving.

ROCKY ROAD BARS

Ingredients

150g/ 5oz gluten free digestive biscuits or Graham Crackers
350g/ 12oz dark chocolate, broken into squares
100g/ 3½ oz unsalted butter, cubed
100g/ 3½ oz mini marshmallows
100g/ 3½ oz glacé cherries/ candied cherries
100g/ 3½ oz chopped nuts
3tbsp golden syrup/ corn syrup

Method

Line and grease a medium sized baking tray with baking paper/ baking parchment.

Put biscuits/crackers into a freezer bag and hit with a rolling pin until they're broken into small pieces. Be sure to leave plenty of chunky pieces, and not beat into crumbs!

In a large pan gently melt the chocolate, butter and golden syrup/ corn syrup, stirring constantly until chocolate has melted. Then set aside. Add the marshmallows, cherries, nuts and biscuit pieces and mix well.

Pour the mixture into the baking tray and spread evenly.

Chill for at least 90 minutes then cut into squares and serve

FLAPJACKS

Ingredients

150g/ 5oz gluten-free oats
60g/ 2oz brown sugar
60g/ 2oz butter
2 tbsp golden syrup/ corn syrup

Method

Preheat the oven to 180C / 350F / Gas Mark 4

Grease and line a 15cm/ 6" square tin.

Over a medium heat, melt the butter, sugar and golden syrup/ corn syrup. Mix in the oats and make sure they're coated thoroughly.

Transfer into the tin, spread evenly and press down firmly.

Bake for approximately 15 minutes or until golden brown.

LEMON & RASPBERRY CUPCAKES

Ingredients

CUPCAKES:

225g/ 8oz gluten free plain / all-purpose flour
225g/ 8oz sugar
150g/ 5oz unsalted butter, room temperature
100ml/ 3½ fl oz buttermilk*
3 large eggs, room temperature
1 tsp vanilla essence
½ tsp lemon essence
¼ tsp bicarbonate of soda/ baking soda
a pinch of salt
zest of one lemon
handful of fresh raspberries, chopped

BUTTERCREAM:

450g/ 1lb icing/ confectioners sugar, sifted
125g/ 4oz cream cheese, chilled and cubed
100g/ 3½ oz unsalted butter, room temperature
½ tsp vanilla essence
fresh raspberries to decorate

Method

Preheat the oven to 180C / 350F / Gas Mark 4

Lightly grease a 12-cup muffin pan or line with paper liners.

For the cupcakes, mix the sugar and lemon zest and leave to infuse for 10 minutes. Beat the sugar and butter until fluffy. Add the eggs one by one and mix well. Add in the vanilla and lemon essences.

In a separate bowl mix the flour and bicarbonate of soda/ baking soda and the salt. Then add this to the butter mixture and mix. Add the buttermilk and mix well. Make sure all the dry ingredients are well combined by folding in.

Divide the mixture between the muffin cases filling around ¾ full. Bake for around 20 minutes or until a skewer comes out clean. Remove from oven to cool on wire rack.

For the buttercream, beat butter until light and fluffy. Add the cream cheese gradually and then sift in the icing/ confectioners sugar. Add the vanilla essence and whisk until light and fluffy. Pipe or spread icing onto the cooled cupcakes and top with a fresh raspberry to serve.

**To make your own buttermilk, simply sour some milk by adding some acid. Pour 250ml milk into a jug and stir in one 15ml tablespoon of lemon juice or white wine vinegar. Stir well and leave to stand for 5 minutes before using as directed in the recipe. Full fat (whole) milk works best.*

BANANA CREAM CUPCAKES

Ingredients

175g/ 6oz almond flour
100g/ 3oz icing / confectioners sugar, sifted
60g/ 2oz vegetable shortening
225g/ 8oz soft cheese
100g/ 3½ oz honey
60g/ 2oz butter, softened
2 large eggs
1-2 ripe mashed bananas + 1 extra banana for decoration, sliced
1 tbsp cornflour/ cornstarch
a pinch of salt
¼ tsp bicarbonate soda/ baking soda
Cinnamon to dust

Method

Preheat the oven to 180C / 350F / Gas Mark 4

Lightly grease a 12-cup muffin pan or line with paper liners.

Combine the almond flour, bicarbonate of soda/ baking soda, cornflour/ cornstarch and salt.

In a separate bowl, mix the eggs, shortening and honey, then stir.

In a large bowl, mix together almond flour, salt and in a smaller bowl combine the eggs, shortening and honey, stir in mashed bananas and then mix with dry ingredients.

Divide the mixture between the muffin cases, filling around ¾ full. Bake for approximately 15 minutes. When cooked remove from oven, allow to cool.

To make the frosting, beat together the butter, soft cheese and icing sugar/ confectioners sugar. Pipe or spread on cupcakes.

Top with a couple of pieces of fresh banana and then dust with cinnamon.

The banana will brown, so only add this if serving immediately.

GINGERBREAD MEN

Ingredients

100g/ 3½ oz brown rice flour
100g/ 3½ oz gluten free plain / all-purpose flour
100g/ 3½ oz sugar
60g/ 2oz shortening
2 tbsp black treacle/ molasses
1 tsp xanthan gum
1 tsp ground ginger
¾ tsp vanilla essence
½ tsp bicarbonate of soda/ baking soda
½ tsp salt
1 large egg
Icing for decoration

Method

Preheat the oven to 190C / 375F / Gas Mark 5
Lightly grease a baking tray.

Combine the sugar, black treacle/ molasses and shortening and beat together. Add all remaining ingredients and beat well. The dough will form so it's soft and pliable.

Roll out the dough on a lightly floured surface to ½cm/ 1/8" thick.

Cut out your gingerbread men with a cutter and place them on the baking tray.

Bake for 6-7 minutes or until the edges are just browning. Remove from oven and let cook on the tray on a wire rack.

Decorate when cooled.

MINCE PIES

Ingredients

75g/ 3oz rice flour
120g/ 4oz gluten free plain / all-purpose flour
175g/ 6oz raisins
100g/ 3oz dried apricots
100g/ 3oz dried cherries
75g/ 3oz dried cranberries
75g/ 3oz unsalted butter, chilled and cubed
4 tbsp sugar
100ml/ 3½ fl oz fresh orange juice
1 banana, mashed
2 tbsp golden syrup/ corn syrup
1 tsp vanilla essence
1 tsp ground cinnamon
¼ tsp grated nutmeg
¼ tsp of allspice
2 tbsp brandy
Icing sugar/ confectioners sugar to decorate

Method

Preheat the oven to 180C / 350F / Gas Mark 4

Lightly grease a 12-cup muffin pan or line with paper liners.

For the filling, put the dried fruit, banana, golden syrup/corn syrup, orange juice, spices and brandy into a bowl, mix well, and leave covered in the fridge overnight for the flavours to develop.

To make the pastry, mix the flour and sugar in a bowl then, using your fingertips, rub the butter through until the mixture resembles breadcrumbs.

Add the vanilla and then mix in 2-3 tbsp of cold water and work this all into a dough. Wrap in clingfilm/ plastic wrap and chill in the fridge for 30 minutes.

When chilled, roll out the pastry on a lightly floured surface and using a pastry cutter or glass tumbler, cut out 12 rounds for bases. Then using a star cutter, cut out 12 lids. Place the bases in the tin, fill with fruit mix then top with a lid.

Brush with some milk before baking for 15 minutes or until golden in colour.

Cool in tins and dust with icing sugar/ confectioners sugar before serving.

CHOCOLATE MOUSSE

Ingredients

300g/ 11oz semi- sweet chocolate
300ml/ 10 fl oz double cream/ heavy cream
3 tbsp unsalted butter
1 tsp gelatin
1 tbsp vanilla essence

Method

Whip 240ml/8 fl oz of the cream and put into fridge to chill. Put the remaining 60ml/ 2 fl oz aside.

In a heatproof bowl over a pot of simmering water melt the chocolate, butter and vanilla. Remove from heat and stir until smooth then let cool to room temperature.

Slightly warm the 60ml/ 2 fl oz of cream and add the gelatin. Let it sit and bloom for approximately 5-10 minutes, then fold into the chocolate mixture.

Fold the whipped cream into the chocolate mixture.

Pour into individual ramekins, if desired, then place in fridge to set.

Decorate as desired.

EASY WHITE BREAD

Ingredients

1kg/ 2¼lb gluten free plain / all-purpose flour
750ml/ 1½ pint whole milk/ full fat milk
1¼ tbsp quick yeast
4 tbsp sugar
6 tbsp oil
4 large eggs
2 tsp vinegar
1 tsp salt

Method

Preheat the oven to 220C / 425F / Gas Mark 7

Grease or line a 1kg/ 2lb bread tin.

Mix together the flour, salt, yeast and sugar.

In a separate bowl beat together the egg, milk and vinegar then add in the dry ingredients and mix well.

Spoon the oil over the mixture and, using your hands, mix together to make into a soft ball of dough. Put the dough into the tin and leave to rise for 60 minutes in a warm place. Sprinkle with sunflower or other seeds, if desired.

Bake in a pre heated oven for 50-55 minutes or until top is golden.

Printed in Great Britain
by Amazon

57393471R00026